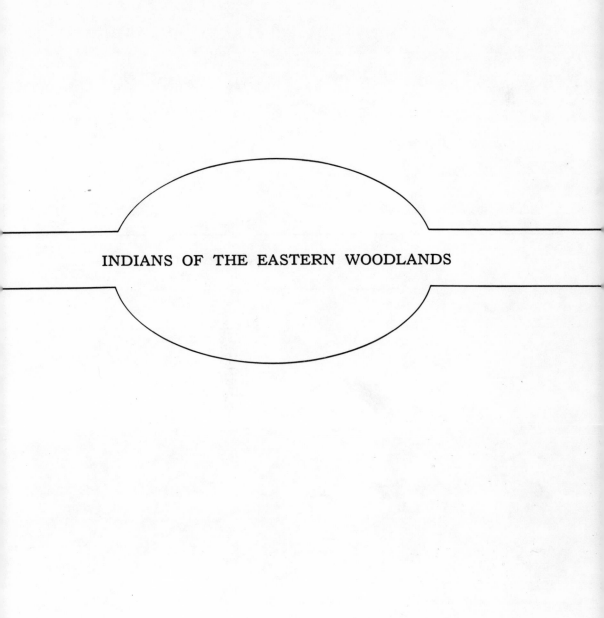

INDIANS OF THE EASTERN WOODLANDS

FRANKLIN WATTS | NEW YORK | LONDON

INDIANS
OF
THE

EASTERN
WOODLANDS

SALLY SHEPPARD

◄ A FIRST BOOK ►

Pictures courtesy of:

Abrams Photo Graphics, Phoenix, Arizona: 82; The American Heritage Publishing Company, © 1961: 28; The American Museum of Natural History: 54; British Library Board, Add. MS. 5253, f. 18: 60; The Haskell Institute and the U.S. Department of Interior, Bureau of Indian Affairs, © 1945: 23; Kahonhes and *Akwesasne Notes*: 37; Oliver La-Farge and Crown Publishers, Inc., © 1956: 24; Library of Congress: 18, 59, 63, 69; American Anthropological Association and The Macmillan Company, © 1966: 13; New-York Historical Society, New York City: 14; The New York Public Library, Picture Collection: 7, 50 (and New York State Historical Association), 70, 76, and Rare Book Division, Astor, Lenox and Tilden Foundations: 20; New York State Museum and Science Service: 4, 33; Tom Porter and Gannett Rochester Newspapers: 79; The Public Archives of Canada: 75; Rochester Museum of Arts and Science Center: 3, 53; Smithsonian Institution National Anthropological Archives, Bureau of American Ethnology Collection: 34, 64; The Traveler's Insurance Co.: 8.

Cover design by Paul Gamarello

Library of Congress Cataloging in Publication Data

Sheppard, Sally.
    Indians of the eastern woodlands.

    (A First book)
    SUMMARY: Discusses the origins, history, and way of life of the Indians of the northeastern United States before and after the arrival of the white man.
    Bibliography: p.
    1. Indians of North America—Juvenile literature. 2. Iroquois Indians—Juvenile literature. 3. Algonquian Indians—Juvenile literature. [1. Indians of North America. 2. Iroquois Indians. 3. Alonquian Indians] I. Title.
E77.4.S49   970.1   74-13609
ISBN 0-531-00825-8

7 6 5 4 3

CONTENTS

The People
1

Family, Clan, Tribe, and Nation
10

A Way of Life
16

Wampum
26

A Government of and by the People
30

A World of Many Spirits
37

Shamans
43

Myths and Legends
45

Heroes and Leaders
48

Woodland Music and Art
52

The White Man Arrives to Stay and Conquer
57

Treaties with the Indians
67

Reservation Life Today
73

Indian Power
78

Looking into the Future
81

Selected Reading
84

Index
86

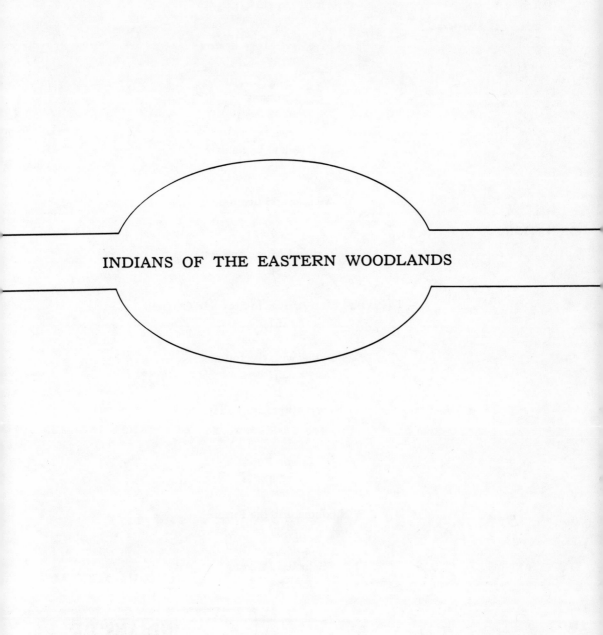

INDIANS OF THE EASTERN WOODLANDS

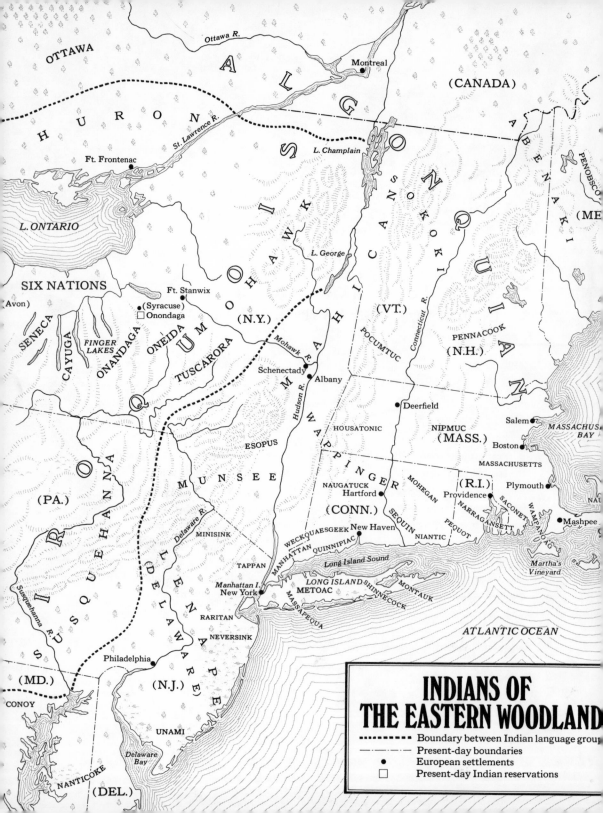

OTTAWA

Ottawa R.

ALGO

Montreal

(CANADA)

HURON

St. Lawrence R.

L. Champlain

Ft. Frontenac

N

L. ONTARIO

O
H
A
W
K

L. George

ABENAKI

(ME

SIX NATIONS

(Avon)

SENECA

CAYUGA

FINGER
LAKES

ONANDAGA

ONEIDA

Ft. Stanwix

(Syracuse)

Onondaga

(N.Y.)

TUSCARORA

U
M

Q

S
O
K
O
K
I

Connecticut R.

(VT.)

PENNACOOK

(N.H.)

Mohawk R.

Schenectady

Albany

Deerfield

Salem

MASSACHUS
BAY

POCUMTUC

HOUSATONIC

NIPMUC

(MASS.)

Boston

ESOPUS

MASSACHUSETTS

(R.I.)

Plymouth

S
U
S
Q
U
E
H
A
N
N
A

I
R
O

(PA.)

M
A
H
I
C
A
N

W
A
P
P
I
N
G
E
R

Hudson R.

MUNSEE

NAUGATUCK

Hartford

(CONN.)

MOHEGAN

SEQUIN

Providence

NARRAGANSETT

NAU

Mashpee

SACONET

W
A
M
P
A
N
O
A
G

R
U

Delaware R.

MINISINK

New Haven

WECKQUAESGEEK

QUINNIPIAC

NIANTIC

PEQUOT

Martha's
Vineyard

TAPPAN

Manhattan

Long Island Sound

D
E
L
A
W
A
R
E

Manhattan I.

New York

LONG ISLAND
METOAC

SHINNECOCK

MONTAUK

RARITAN

MASSAPEQUA

ATLANTIC OCEAN

NEVERSINK

Philadelphia

(N.J.)

(MD.)

CONOY

UNAMI

Delaware
Bay

NANTICOKE

(DEL.)

INDIANS OF
THE EASTERN WOODLAND

- - - - Boundary between Indian language group
— · — · Present-day boundaries
● European settlements
□ Present-day Indian reservations

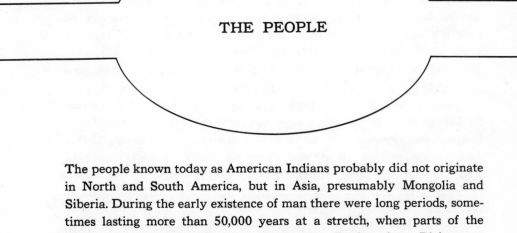

THE PEOPLE

The people known today as American Indians probably did not originate in North and South America, but in Asia, presumably Mongolia and Siberia. During the early existence of man there were long periods, sometimes lasting more than 50,000 years at a stretch, when parts of the earth were covered with great ice masses. During these Pleistocene glacial periods there were portions of the earth where plant and animal life flourished making it possible for man to subsist. It is believed that the Bering Strait was once land and possibly a fertile, grassy plain. We do know that Alaska was not always dominated by snow and ice.

It is impossible to set exact dates for the migration of Asian peoples to the Americas, but we do know that man was in Mexico and the southwestern United States as early as 20,000 years ago, and in the eastern United States some five thousand years later. In 1973 archaeologists found new evidence of man's existence in the American Southwest over

200,000 years ago. Nomadic people, men, women, and children, lived where wild game and vegetation were fast becoming scarce. Their own land was slowly becoming enveloped in snow and ice and ever-lowering temperatures. There was only one solution for these people — to move. So, slowly they began to follow the herds and to seek fertile valleys and plains. Since the animals were moving east it was obvious that was the direction to take.

A glacier may be many miles wide and as much as one thousand feet thick but it moves very, very slowly. Between two glaciers may be miles of valleys which will support plant and animal life. It is probable that these people roamed these valleys in their search for survival.

Eventually some of the people reached what is now the southwestern part of the United States which, at that time, was free of glaciers. As their population increased they fanned out — some going all the way south into South and Central America, some crossing from west to east, eventually reaching the eastern coast of the United States. These people are the ancestors of many of the Indians of the eastern woodlands, particularly the Algonquian-speaking tribes. Some scientists believe that the Iroquoian-speaking Indians came to upstate New York and the Great Lakes region from the north rather than a migration from the south. One must not assume that any of these migrations, including those from Asia, were in terms of thousands of persons at a time. Populations were small in those times and probably little groups of a few families or tribes moved almost without realizing it.

Due to archaeological explorations or "digs," certain implements, various artifacts, and even bones can give the trained "digger" a fair picture of the people who lived in the area. Archaeologists have discovered certain artifacts and remnants of civilizations which, with expert know-how, can be reconstructed to give us a good idea of life in those early times. Sometimes human bones are found and from even a few, a physical anthropologist can draw a picture of what that man or woman may have looked like. So, we can tell whether they were short or tall and whether their faces were broad or long. Since we are concerned only with the Indians of the eastern woodlands — from just west of the Hudson River to the Atlantic coast and from New York and

EXCAVATION OF AN EARLY BURIAL
IN CENTRAL NEW YORK STATE.
THESE PEOPLE WERE FARMERS
WHO ALSO HUNTED AND FISHED.

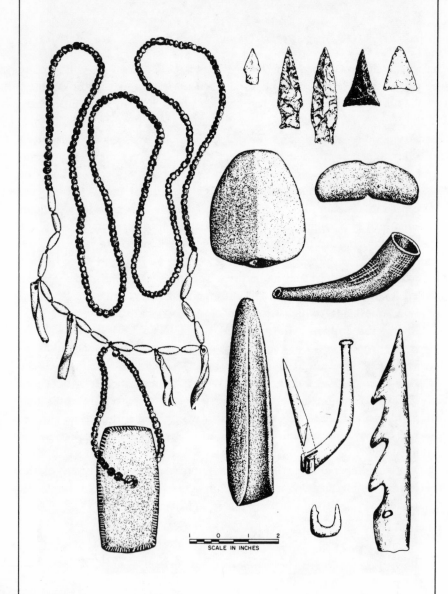

SCALE IN INCHES

PREHISTORIC TOOLS, WEAPONS,
AND ORNAMENTS FOUND IN
THE EASTERN ALGONQUIAN AREA.

eastern Pennsylvania north to the Canadian border — we will confine ourselves to those early migrants who settled in this part of the country.

This book is mainly about the historic times, just prior to the coming of the Europeans and during their exploration and contact with the land and its peoples, the Indians. The history of the Indians of the eastern woodlands is complicated by the fact that there were many tribes who had similar cultures, but which did differ in varying degrees. Some of the descendants of these tribes still live today, but many tribes have disappeared. To simplify things we will divide the eastern woodland Indians into two main groups based on their language roots. They are the Algonquians and the Iroquois. It might be pointed out now that the name "Indian" is the white man's word because he believed when he first came to the Americas that he had reached the East Indies and therefore called its inhabitants "Indians." Today many Indians prefer to be called "native Americans," which is indeed closer to the truth.

Among the Indians who migrated to the New York area were the Lenape (pronounced *Lay-nap-e*), whom today we refer to as the Delaware. There is a tradition among the Delaware Indians called the *Walum Olum* or Painted Score. The Walum Olum, which is of questionable authenticity, but nonetheless interesting, is a written interpretation of pictographs. These are primitive drawings often depicting current events, history, and legend. When found on rocks they are called petroglyphs.

Delaware legend says the Walum Olum depicts the history of the people. A small portion of the Walum Olum as translated by D. G. Brinton of Philadelphia during the late 1800s, says:

After the rushing waters,
The Lenarpe of the Turtle
Were close together in hollow homes
It freezes where they abode
It snows, it storms, it is cold where they abode.
All the cabin fires in that land were disquieted
And all said to their Priest
LET US GO

On the wonderful slippery water
On the stone hard water
All went.
On the great tidal sea,
The mussel-bearing sea,
They all come.
They tarry at the land of the spruce pines
Those from the West
Come with hesitation
Esteeming highly their old home at the Turtle land.

If the Walum Olum is real then Delaware tradition substantiates our belief that the Indians originated in a hard, cold, and stormy land.

In 1665 a European, David Pieterz de Vries, described the Indians, saying: "The Indians about were all tolerably stout, have black hair, wear a long lock which they let hang on one side of the head. The hair is shorn at the top like a cockscomb. Some of the women are very well featured, have a long countenance...." Both Iroquois and Algonquians were brown-eyed and olive- to reddish-skinned, although there were Indians in the northern coastal regions whose skin was much lighter than we generally associate with Indian appearance. The Indians were well proportioned and physically well developed. They were agile, swift runners and had exceptionally keen senses of sight and hearing. They were capable of great physical endurance and from early childhood were trained to the rigors of an active and outdoor life, particularly the boys.

It was not until unscrupulous white men began to treat them badly that they began to make war on the intruders. Not all white men were unkind and unfair to Indians nor were all Indians always on the warpath against the settlers and traders. The Indians were trying to protect that which they considered theirs and the white man was here to colonize and gain riches. The two goals were bound to clash, often to the detriment of both white and Indian, but finally to the subjugation and eventual disinheritance of the Indians.

Among the Iroquois-speaking people were the Senecas, Oneidas, Cayugas, Onondagas, and the Mohawks. It was Indians of the Algon-

A WARRIOR WITH BODY PAINT AND BOW,
DRAWN IN THE SIXTEENTH CENTURY.

THE EXPLORER ADRIAEN BLOCK'S
SHIP PASSES INDIANS ON THE
CONNECTICUT SHORE IN 1614.

quian tongue who greeted the Pilgrims and other earlier settlers to eastern shores. Included among them were the Mahicans of New York State, the Mohegans of Connecticut, the Narragansetts of Rhode Island, the Wampanoags of Massachusetts, and the Passamaquoddys and Penobscots of Maine. This is not a complete list of tribes, but the names of some of the most powerful and influential. On Long Island, for example, were Shinnecocks and Montauks, and there were others, such as the Pequots, Quinnipiacs, and Naugatucks, in other parts of New York and New England. Many of today's names of towns, cities, and villages are derived from or actually named for the Indians who once inhabited the areas.

FAMILY, CLAN, TRIBE, AND NATION

Although the basic family of father, mother, and children was common to both Iroquois and Algonquian cultures, there were differences in their relationship to the social structure as a whole.

Both groups had a matriarchal society, but it was much stronger among the Iroquois. In a matriarchal society the woman is the pivotal point. For example, an Iroquois son did not inherit his father's property, but he could inherit from his mother, his mother's brothers and sisters, or a grandfather on his mother's side. When his mother and father were married they lived with his mother's tribe or clan.

After the family came the clan, but the Algonquians of New York probably had no clan. The clan was an extension of the family to include blood relatives through the mother's side of the family. The Iroquois had such clan names as Turtle, Wolf, Deer, Snipe, etc. Every member of a clan considered himself a brother to every other member and marriage within a clan was not allowed. The tribe could consist of several clans and as a group lived within the confines of a village or settlement. A clan could number up to two hundred persons and was dominated by an elder woman. She was not necessarily the oldest, but was chosen for her wisdom and for the respect in which she was held by clan members.

Women exercised considerable power because it was the women who chose from their families the chiefs and tribal leaders. If the women were displeased with a leader's performance they could depose him and appoint another in his place. When a chief was appointed he took the name of his predecessor, giving up his own given name. Chiefs might change, but the name remained the same. Among the Iroquois, women were never chiefs, but their influence was strongly felt and they were truly the "power behind the throne."

The Algonquians of New York also had a matriarchal society, but it was seemingly not as rigid as the Iroquois. There the men apparently had more power in the political and social affairs. The chief or *sachem* as he was called, inherited his position and it was possible for a woman to attain the title if there were no male descendants in the direct line of succession.

The social structure of the Iroquois Indians is considerably confusing. For instance, an Indian child had a real mother and father. If the mother had sisters they were also called "mother" by the child. Likewise, if the grandmother on the mother's side had sisters, they were also the same child's grandmothers. If the mother's sister had children they were not known as cousins, but as brothers and sisters. If the father had a sister her children were his nieces and nephews, but his sister's grandchildren were also his grandchildren. These were the chief relatives within the tribe, all related through the female line. However, outside the tribe a grandfather on the father's side was a grandfather, as were his brothers, and the children could also call their father's brothers "father."

There was little chance of being without relatives and even today many Indians still cling somewhat to the custom and refer to relatives by names of closer kinship than generally accepted by the white man.

Families and clans were subdivisions of a tribe, and each nation was made up of several tribes — all related by blood or marriage. Among

(11)

the Five Nations of the Iroquois, the Senecas, Cayugas, and Onondagas had eight tribes each, while the Oneidas and the Mohawks had but three. The eight tribes were divided into two divisions — the first division included Wolf, Bear, Beaver, and Turtle and the second included Deer, Snipe, Heron, and Hawk. Marriage laws were very strict and men and women of the first division could not marry each other. The same applied to the second division. Therefore, a man from the Wolf tribe could marry a woman from Deer, Snipe, Heron, or Hawk, but he could not marry a woman from Bear. All members of each tribe considered themselves "brothers" of any tribe of the same name. For example, an Onondaga of Wolf tribe looked upon the Mohawk of the Wolf tribe as his brother. Among the tribes of the same name in each nation were actual blood ties. Even today modern members of the Six Nations of the Iroquois League (the Tuscaroras joined about 1715, making six nations) still cling to these tribal names and divisions and still feel strongly about their "brother" relationship each with the other. Loyalties within family, clan, tribe, and nation were very strong and the Indian practiced the philosophy of "I am my brother's keeper." If a child were orphaned, he was quickly cared for by relatives or friends and it was considered a great honor and particularly pleasing to the Great Spirit to care for an orphan child.

Among the Algonquian Indians the family was the basic unit of society and very often brothers and their wives, grandparents, and cousins lived under the same roof. Their tribes were composed of a group of families with a headman or sachem as the leader.

There was one outstanding difference between the Algonquian and Iroquois Indians. Among the New England coastal Indians, including the Mohegans, the Pequots, Penobscots, Massachusetts, etc., lineage was derived through the father. Clans did exist and marriage was generally outside the clan, in which case the wife went to live with her husband's people, unlike the Iroquois who lived with the wife's people.

All the Indian tribes had a strong family feeling and one was expected to keep track of his relatives, perhaps as many as fifty to sixty.

The Algonquian Indians were basically monogamous, taking only one wife. However, if they could afford to pay the bridal tribute for more

YOUR LONGHOUSE FAMILY

 Members of your father's longhouse family

 Members of your (your mother's) longhouse family

Notice that not all members of your longhouse family live in your longhouse
and not all the people in your longhouse are members of your longhouse family.

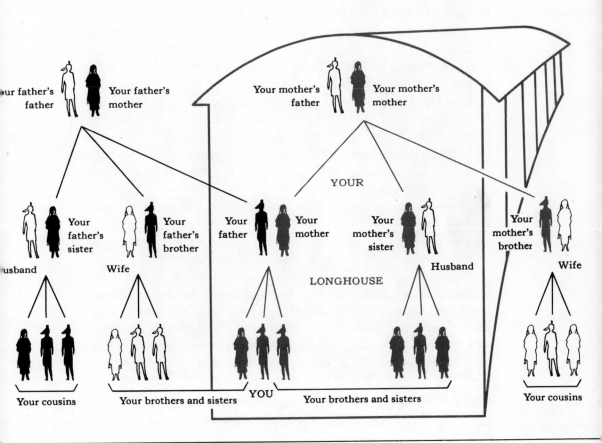

Your father's father   Your father's mother   Your mother's father   Your mother's mother

YOUR

Your father's sister   Your father's brother   Your father   Your mother   Your mother's sister   Your mother's brother

Husband   Wife   Husband   Wife

LONGHOUSE

Your cousins   Your brothers and sisters   YOU   Your brothers and sisters   Your cousins

MOHAWK CHIEF HO-NEE-YEATH-TAN-NO-RON
OF THE WOLF TRIBE, PAINTED ABOUT 1710.

than one wife, they were permitted to do so. If a man was dissatisfied with his wife, he was at liberty to send her away. The marriage ceremony was a simple affair of the bridegroom presenting gifts to the bride's mother or parents. Like the Iroquois, the Algonquian couple, while married to each other, were expected to remain faithful or suffer severe punishment. Among the Iroquois more than one wife was uncommon, but divorce was allowed although it was frowned upon. The mother and women members of the wife's family were expected to mediate and settle differences between a couple.

A WAY OF LIFE

The life style of the eastern woodland Indian was basically one of hunting, fishing, gathering of nuts, fruits, and berries, eventually raising such crops as corn, beans, tobacco, squash, sweet potatoes. Corn, squash, and beans were the main staples of the Indian diet and were called the "three sisters." Tobacco had a sacred and ceremonial use as the smoke was believed able to carry messages and prayers to the various spirits. The pursuit of food and its storage was paramount in Indian life. Severe winters, floods, or droughts could easily mean death.

The houses of the east coast tribes, the Wampanoags, the Mohegans, the Passamaquoddys, and others, were built in a conical or round shape with a frame of saplings bent to form the shape and fastened together. Over this frame pieces of tree bark were overlapped to provide protection from the elements. Sizes varied from ten to more than thirty feet in diameter. Over the overlapping bark was a thatch of grass. A small hole at the top allowed smoke from the fires to escape. The edges of the hole in the roof were daubed with clay for fire protection. Beds were matting covered with animal skins and a small depression in the center of the floor was for the cooking fire which also furnished heat and light. The dome-shaped wigwam was common on eastern Long Island and in the Hudson Valley. One of Henry Hudson's men described a house:

A house well constructed of oak bark and circular in shape, so that they had the appearance of being built with an arched roof. It contained a great quantity of maize or Indian corn and beans of last year's growth, and there lay near the house for the purpose of drying enough to load three ships, besides what was growing in the fields. On our coming into the house, two mats were spread out to sit upon, and immediately some food was served in well made red wooden bowls; two men were also dispatched at once with bows and arrows in quest of game, who after brought in a pair of pigeons which they had shot.

The longhouse structure prominent on western Long Island was a rectangle from twenty to one hundred feet long and usually housed several families. Each family had its own fire. The floor of the longhouse was earth and the sides and roof were made of reed and the bark of chestnut trees. The frames were tree limbs driven into the ground and fastened together. The roof was raised about six inches in order to let smoke escape. The roofs were very low and doors were so narrow and low that one had to stoop and squeeze himself through.

Cooking utensils included clay and wooden pots, bowls, calabashes (gourds), and spoons made from gourds.

Ten to eleven thousand years ago, the first Indians were able to hunt such animals as mastodon, musk-ox, great beaver, elk, moose, and caribou. For hunting these animals during this Paleolithic period, the Indians used a spear with a fluted edge. They had crude knives for butchering the animals and simple instruments to scrape and cure the hides. As the glacier receded, some of the wild game, such as the mastodon, musk-ox, and caribou, became extinct in the northeastern states. In historic times there were deer, bear, turkey, waterfowl, fish, and shellfish for those in coastal regions. Indians also ate dogs, snakes, frogs, eagles, skunks, and

IROQUOIS OF THE SEVENTEENTH CENTURY
DRIVING GAME INTO A TRAP
BY STRIKING BONES TOGETHER.

fox. Mealtime was whenever one got hungry. Fires were made with a wooden drill rotated between the hands. Occasionally the prehistoric method of striking sparks from a tinder was used.

The Algonquians' hunting and fighting weapons were bows with flint or bone-tipped arrows, spears, and clubs. Traps and snares were also used to capture game. Fishhooks were made of bone, as were fishing spears. Fishnets and weirs were also employed by coastal Indians.

Transportation was on foot over land and by dugout canoe and later birchbark canoe where this bark was available. Snowshoes, dogsleds, and toboggans were used for overland travel in the winter.

In the summertime the Algonquians wore a simple loincloth made of deerskin. The heads of the men were shaved except for a long scalplock. During the cold months they wore leggings made of animal skins.

The Iroquois tribes lived much the same as the Algonquian tribes except that they did not have the advantage of a seacoast, but they did have Lake Erie and Lake Ontario. Like the land of the Algonquians, there were many rivers and lakes where fish were abundant. There were also fertile valleys for raising crops and hunting buffalo. The forest provided fresh meat such as deer, bear, wildfowl, and small game animals.

Their houses differed from those of the coastal Algonquians. They used longhouses but they were usually larger than the longhouses of the Algonquian tribes. Sometimes these longhouses could hold as many as ten families. Within the longhouse each family had its own fire where the women prepared the meals. The longhouse was also woven into the religion and government of the Iroquois people, as we shall see in later chapters. The Iroquois also used bark houses which they called gä-nó-sote, but the house we associate with Iroquois culture is the longhouse. Very often Iroquois villages were enclosed by rows of palisades, fences made of stakes, sharpened and driven into the ground.

Indian settlements were usually near adequate supplies of water, very often on lakeshores. Like the Algonquians, the Iroquois used a dugout canoe because the proper birchbark was not available in the forests of northwestern New York.

For the Iroquois the bow and arrow was the major hunting equipment, although blow guns were used for squirrels and small birds. Trap-

AN IROQUOIS VILLAGE
SHOWING LONGHOUSES AND FIELDS
AND DAILY ACTIVITIES.

ping was also employed and fish were caught by traps, weirs, nets, and sometimes hooks and lines. Freshwater clams were also part of the Iroquois diet. For most of the year the men hunted in the woods surrounding their villages, but after the fall harvest hunting parties of small family groups would travel farther afield to camp and hunt for several months. Women accompanied the hunters to prepare the meat for storing and the hides for clothing and bedding. The Iroquois Indians, as did their Algonquian neighbors, collected maple sap in the spring. Corn, beans, and squash were also the staples of the Iroquois diet. To store their surplus corn, they dug a pit, lined its bottom and sides with bark, and covered it with a bark roof tightly fitted for waterproofing. After the corn was deposited the pit was covered with earth. Cured venison and other meats were buried in the same way, except that the bark pit was lined with deerskin.

Many of the vegetables which the Indian introduced to white settlers were originally native wild plants which they had domesticated. Corn, which one associates with Indian food and agriculture, probably originated in Central America. This is another piece of evidence that the eastern woodland Indians came originally from the south, possibly Mexico or New Mexico and Arizona. At least the presence of corn in New England and New York shows that they had some contact with people from Central America. It would seem that they must have used corn as a staple food and for that reason brought seed corn with them as they started their migration eastward.

Like the Algonquians, the Iroquois were very hospitable people. Houses were never locked and always open for travelers. Strangers were welcome and food was always provided. When visiting an Iroquois home, one was always expected to at least taste the food offered and to say *Hi-ne-ä'-weh* — I thank you. According to Louis Henry Morgan, a nineteenth-century scientist who lived with the Iroquois: "He [an Iroquois] would surrender his dinner to feed the hungry, vacate his bed to refresh the weary, and give up his apparel to clothe the naked." Various kinds of tea were served by Iroquois women. One of the favorites was made from the boiled tips of hemlock boughs and served with maple sugar.

Maple tea was made by boiling sap and seasoning it with sassafras root. Teas were concocted by steeping wild spices.

By the nineteenth century the dress of the Iroquois Indian had reached a highly sophisticated and decorative appearance. The women's skirts were long and elaborately decorated with beadwork. Of course, the blue broadcloth favored by Iroquois women was a product of their trade relations with the white men. In ancient times the women wore deerskin leggings embroidered with porcupine quills. These eventually gave way to the red broadcloth and beadwork replaced the porcupine quills. A long-sleeved round-necked overdress completed the women's costume. Often these too were highly decorated, sometimes with silver. Iroquois women were fond of jewelry and many wore earrings, rings, and beads and, following the incursion of Christian missionaries, sometimes crosses. Cradleboards for infants which were carried by the mother on her back, were extremely elaborate, occasionally intricately carved and the skin coverings worked in beadwork designs.

Arnoldus Montanus wrote in 1671 that:

The women ornament themselves more than the men. The men wear between the legs a lap of cloth or leather [loincloth]. . . . The women wear a petticoat midway down the leg, very richly ornamented with seawant [wampum] so that the garments sometimes cost 300 guilders. They also wrap the naked body in a deerskin — the edges of which swing with fringe. A long robe fastened at the right shoulder by a knot, at the waist by a girdle, served the men and women for an upper ornament and by night for a bedcover. Both go for the most part bareheaded. . . . Moccasins and leggings were made of elk hides. . . .

In the cold winter both Algonquians and Iroquois used the skins of fur-bearing animals for warmth in their dress. Many of the Algonquian tribes made capes of overlapping wild turkey feathers which provided protection from the rain and cold.

Indian children were dearly loved by their parents and relatives and discipline was administered firmly but lovingly. Spanking or hitting children was almost unheard of in Indian families, but a naughty child

A NINETEENTH-CENTURY SENECA WOMAN
POUNDING CORN, A STAPLE FOOD
OF THE EASTERN WOODLANDS.

IROQUOIS COSTUME FOR WOMAN,
CHILD, AND MAN FOR THE LATE
EIGHTEENTH–EARLY NINETEENTH CENTURIES.

might have cold water thrown in his face as punishment. Children were taught great respect for their elders, families, and clans and to do wrong was to bring shame to their families.

Children were given toys, but more often than not these toys were "teaching" toys. A boy might be given a small bow and arrow or spear to learn the rudiments of hunting and warfare. Dolls and miniature household implements were given to little girls to instruct them in the care of their future families. Sometimes the dolls were made from corn husks and occasionally carved from wood. Girls were also taught how to plant seed and gather crops for that was considered women's work, while hunting, fishing, and warfare were left to the men.

When a boy approached adolescence he was usually sent into the wilderness to prove that he could survive and take his place among the men. During this lonely time in the forest he was also encouraged to remember any visions or dreams which might come to him. When he returned to his family, he often reported that he had had visions giving him a new name. Sometimes the dreams were interpreted by others and from these interpretations a new name was given to the young man and the name of his childhood discarded. Once he had successfully completed his endurance feat he took his rightful place among adult tribe members, but always mindful of the respect due his elders.

As girls approached womanhood they were also sent away, usually to a hut to fast and hopefully to have visions which would give them new names and provide guidance for the future.

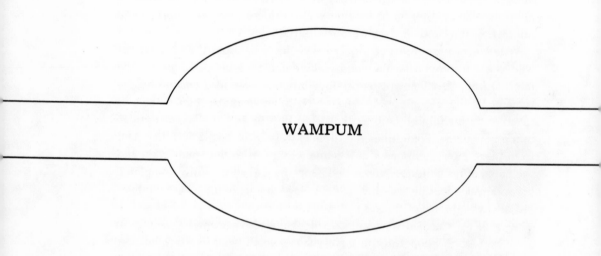

WAMPUM

Today when we speak of Indian wampum, we usually think of it in terms of money or an item to be traded for goods. The original meaning of wampum among the northeastern Indians was not money, but was of social, political, and religious significance. There were two kinds of wampum beads. White wampum was made from the inside of the conch, a large saltwater univalve. Dark wampum, which ranged from purple or blue to black, was taken from the quahog, a thick-shelled saltwater clam. The size of the beads was approximately one-quarter inch wide and three-eighths to one-half inches thick. The beads were laced with fiber or narrow strips of deerskin and made into necklaces, bracelets, strings, belts, girdles, and collars. Each bead had a set value, the darkest being worth twice as much as the white.

It was very difficult to make wampum beads. Before the Indians had such advanced tools as awls from Europe, they had to bore out the shell with sharp stones. (Once the Europeans realized the value attached to wampum beads by the Indians they were quick to capitalize by selling the Indians small colored glass beads.) Such tribes as the Iroquois, who used wampum extensively, had to travel sometimes many hundreds of miles to trade with the coastal Indians in order to obtain the saltwater shells. Wampum beads were strung together in such a way that they conveyed certain messages and Indians were able to "read" a wampum belt.

The early settlers found wampum of such value to the Indians that they used it in trading for valuable furs to buy food and other necessities. Rows of black or white wampum on belts represented paths to specific places. The freedom belt of the Iroquois had a white background with purple beads running in a rectangular path across the length of the belt. It represented the idea of freedom, that the Indian reserved the perpetual right to cross whenever necessary lands previously sold to the whites. Wampum belts were also used as records and evidence of treaties, as the Indians never fully accepted pen and ink treaties of the white man. A special officer of the tribe, usually a sachem, was delegated to safeguard wampum belts as a sacred duty.

During council meetings, a speaker holding a belt or string of wampum in his hands would rise and begin his talk. At the end of his speech he would give the wampum to the group he had just addressed. When the belt was presented, the Indians shouted their approval of what had been said. Wampum was also used in almost all Indian diplomacy. It was used in making alliances, preventing disputes, cementing friendships, and assuring future fidelity. Wampum was also a means of identifying a messenger.

In 1742 a powerful Iroquois sachem, Canassatego, with a wampum belt criticized the Delawares for daring to negate land transactions without Iroquois approval:

Let this Belt of Wampum serve to Chastise You; You ought to be taken by the Hair of the Head and Shak'd severely till you recover your Senses and become Sober ... Don't deliberate, but remove away and take this Belt of Wampum ... This String of Wampum serves to

IROQUOIS WAMPUM BELT MADE IN THE
1500s, COMMEMORATING THE UNIFICATION
OF THE FIVE NATIONS IN THE LEAGUE.

Forbid You, Your Children and Grand Children, to the latest Posterity, forever meddling in Land Affairs, neither you nor any who shall descend from You are ever hereafter to presume to sell any Land, for which purpose you are to Preserve this string in Memory of what your Uncles have this Day given You in Charge.

Even today Indians consider wampum a part of their sacred heritage. Not too long ago, at a sale of Indian artifacts and relics at the Sotheby Parke-Bernet Galleries in New York, some wampum was put up for sale. Iroquois Indians of New York State objected strongly to the sale of their sacred wampum and the items were removed from the sale.

A GOVERNMENT OF AND BY THE PEOPLE

Among the Algonquian-speaking peoples there were many tribes. At the head of each tribe were hereditary chiefs or sachems. Their power was not absolute, for each chief had an equal voice in the tribal councils. However, there often emerged an outstanding leader who became the chief sachem. Although his influence could be considerable, he could not act without the consent of all other chiefs of his council. Eventually there developed various confederacies or groups of tribes which banded together for the mutual welfare and protection of their territories from enemies. These confederations were loosely knit and never as well defined and organized as the League of the Iroquois. However, they were useful in times of warfare, and in their confrontation with the white man, were a means to present a united front.

Very often the Iroquois are referred to as the "Greeks of America," for they had a relatively advanced democratic form of government. It was truly of, by, and for the people. The Indian name of the Iroquois was *Ho-dé-no-saw-ne*. The Iroquois peoples in ancient times had been aggressive and warlike, conquering many tribes as far west as the Mississippi River and as far south as Tennessee. The reason for the formation of the League of the Iroquois was to promote peace and self-protection.

Because of the family-clan-tribal setup of the Iroquois, to make war among the Five Nations would have been to make war with one's brothers. This was a strong factor to the lasting quality of the league. The League of Five Nations was formed in 1570 by the Oneidas, Senecas, Mohawks, Cayugas, and Onondagas. According to legend, the idea for the league was that of a refugee from the Huron tribe named *De-gan-a-wi-dah*. Credit for the eventual acceptance of De-gan-a-wi-dah's philosophy of nonviolence is given to *Hiawatha*, a Mohawk chief. (Longfellow mistakenly described Hiawatha as an Ojibwa and placed him in a New England setting.) The final agreement to form a confederacy took several years. Hiawatha and De-gan-a-wi-dah first achieved the cooperation of the friendly nations of the Iroquois and finally were able to persuade *A-te-tcho*, the powerful chieftain of the Onondagas to join the confederacy.

The confederacy council consisted of fifty chiefs whose names have come down to us. The title of De-gan-a-wi-dah is always left vacant out of respect to the legendary founder. There are nine chiefs each from the Mohawk and Oneida nations, ten from the Cayugas, eight from the Senecas, and fourteen from the Onondagas. However, this did not mean that the Onondagas had fourteen votes while the Senecas had only eight. Each nation voted as a unit so actually each nation had but one vote.

However, some of the nations were obviously more powerful than others and therefore were given special rights and responsibilities. The Mohawks, whose territory bordered their traditional enemy, the Algonquins, were made "Keepers of the Eastern Door of the Longhouse." Since the enemy was to the east, they symbolized protection from hostile neighbors. As recognition for their leadership, no league meeting was considered unless the Mohawk confederacy chiefs were present and no motions could be passed over a Mohawk protest. The "Keepers of the Western Door" were the Senecas, who were the westernmost Iroquois nation. The

Onondagas, whose lands were located in the middle, were appointed "Keepers of the Central Fire." They also called meetings, set up the agenda, and the wampum belonging to the league was held traditionally by an Onondaga sachem whose name was *Ho-wo-we-nä'-to*, "Keeper of the Wampum." They had the power of veto, but their veto could be overridden.

Each nation or tribe had a council made up of village chiefs. This tribal council managed tribal affairs and again a decision had to be unanimous to carry. All the confederacy chiefs were men, but they were chosen by the women and could be removed by the women. Sometimes these titles were hereditary within clans. In such cases, the chief matron or elder woman, in consultation with other women of her clan, named a chief. Tenure for a confederacy chief was a lifetime one, unless he became too ill to serve or committed an offense against his people. In addition to the regular members of the council, a group called Pine Tree Chiefs was later set up. These were men or women who had shown outstanding ability and were elected by the council. They could not be removed from office, but if they behaved contrary to Iroquois philosophy, the others turned a deaf ear to them. The Pine Tree Chiefs could voice opinions in the confederacy council, but they had no vote.

The constitution of the Iroquois confederacy provided for direct consultation by council members with the people on matters of grave importance. They were admonished to meet with the people and abide by their decisions. Both men and women members of any clan could bring a matter before the council and they had a right to form committees and appoint delegates to council meetings. The symbol of the confederacy came from the forest — the Great Tree of People. The Great Tree represented the law. The branches symbolized shelter and protection for the people of the league. The white roots of the Great Tree were believed to stretch to the four corners of the earth and that other people would see them and follow them to the protection of the Great Tree. The Iroquois believed that the confederacy might eventually bring all nations of the world to peace.

Watching over the Tree was the "Eagle that Sees Afar." He was to sound the alarm in case of danger. Under the ground beneath the Tree

MODEL OF A COUNCIL OF THE
TURTLE CLAN OF THE ONONDAGA.

RED JACKET OR SHAGOIE'WATHA,
A SENECA WAR CHIEF.

was a cavern with a stream of water. This stream symbolically was to carry away the weapons of war which were thrown into the cavern. Beneath the branches of the Tree was the white mat of the law. Here the council members were to sit when they deliberated.

The council of the League of the Iroquois met once each year, but could be convened at other times if necessary; for instance, if a chief died or was removed from office. When a chief died, his successor was named from the same clan and given the same name.

About 1715, the Tuscaroras, who were an Iroquoian-speaking people driven from their homes in North Carolina, asked for and received homes within the Iroquois League territory. They were represented at the confederacy council by their chiefs, but had no vote. After the admittance of the Tuscaroras, the Five Nations became known as the Six Nations as they are known today.

The constitution of the League of the Iroquois is a remarkable document and to some degree served as a model for the United States Constitution and Bill of Rights. This fact is freely acknowledged by Thomas Jefferson in his autobiography.

In Article 17 were contained the plans of the matriarchal society:

A bunch of a certain number of shell (wampum) strings each two spaces in length shall be given to each of the female families in which the Lordship titles are vested. The rights of bestowing the title shall be hereditary in the family of females legally possessing the bunch of shell strings and the strings shall be the token that the females of the family have the proprietary right to the Lordship title for all time to come, subject to certain restrictions hereinafter mentioned.

The constitution further states in Article 43:

The lineal descent of the people shall run in the female line. Women shall be considered the progenitors of the Nation. They shall own the land and the soil. Men and women shall follow the status of the mother.

The symbol of Lordship or chieftaincy was the antlers of a deer. If a man was seriously ill or dying, the women in authority removed the antlers, but if he recovered, the antlers were placed on his head as a symbol of continuing authority. When a man was conferred as a chief he was expected to supply a feast consisting of cooked venison, corn bread, and corn soup. When a chief died there was a ten-day mourning period during which the council could not sit.

In a section of the constitution entitled, "Rights of the People" (comparable to the United States Bill of Rights), Section 93 states that an emergency or specially important matter must be submitted to the people and the decision of the people shall affect the decision of the confederacy council. This decision shall be a confirmation of the voice of the people. The women of each clan were given the right to have a council fire. Among other rights of the people were the right to delegate power and to report decisions to the council of the nation or the confederacy council, the right to keep council fires, and the right to protest irregularities in the performance of the Great Peace, being the basic philosophy upon which the league was founded. Also guaranteed was the right to hold rites and festivals. A man's home was not to be trespassed against. When a stick or pole was left against a home in a slanting position, this meant that the homeowner was absent and no one was permitted to enter.

The constitution of the Six Nations is a lengthy document, but from these few excerpts it is easy to see that it is an advanced and humane document.

A WORLD OF MANY SPIRITS

All eastern woodland Indians, despite their tribe or language, believed in one Supreme Being. The Iroquois called him *Hä-wen-né-yu*, while among the Algonquians he was known as *Kau-tan-towwit* by the Wampanoags and *Gicelámu-Kaong* by the Delawares. They also believed in an Evil Spirit who was much like the devil in the Christian religion. This god was called *Hä-ne-go-até-geh*, the "Evil-Minded." *Hä-wen-né-yu*, or as the white man called him, the "Great Spirit," was credited with the creation of man and all useful animals and products of the earth, but the Evil Spirit was supposed to have created all monsters, poisonous reptiles, and toxic plants. In other words, the Great Spirit made everything that was good for man and the Evil Spirit created everything that was bad for man.

Some of the Algonquian Indians in New York also believed in a powerful evil god which they called *Mutchesunnetooh*. Another Algonquian people, the Wampanoags of Martha's Vineyard in Massachusetts called their evil god *Ho-bo-mocko-Manitoo.*

All of the tribes made sacrifices and offerings to various spirits for favors such as rain for their crops, good weather, and the expulsion of evil spirits from men and women who were sick or who had committed a wrongdoing, or who were suspected of witchcraft. During most of their religious ceremonies the Indians never burned tobacco in prayers of thanksgiving, but when asking for favors from the Great Spirit or his assistant spirits or invisible aides, they did burn tobacco, believing that the smoke would carry their prayers to the spirit world.

Among the Iroquois there were six regular festivals or thanksgivings. The first was the Maple Festival in the early spring to give thanks to the maple tree for its sap. Next was the Planting Festival where prayers were offered to the Great Spirit to bless the seed. Then came the Strawberry Festival which was thanksgiving for the first fruits of the earth. The fourth festival of the six regular festivals was the Green Corn Festival held for the ripening of the corn, beans, and squash — the three sisters. The next festival was the Harvest Thanksgiving to "Our Supporters" after the gathering of the harvest. This was a thanksgiving to the Great Spirit and to all the forces which had made possible a profitable harvest. The New Year's Festival rounded out the year and during this time a white dog was sacrificed.

All festivals of the Iroquois began with speeches by leaders. During the day several speeches were given by teachers and keepers of the faith. The speeches would include reminders of the virtues which became a warrior, the people's duties as members of a common brotherhood, the duty of living in harmony and peace, to avoid speaking evil, of kindness to orphans, charity to the needy, and hospitality to all.

Following speeches there was usually a dance which was actually considered a form of worship. The Iroquois believed that the Great Spirit knew he could not live without some kind of amusement, therefore, he gave them dancing. The Great Feather Dance of the Iroquois was reserved exclusively for religious councils and for great occasions. The Thunderer, *Hé-no,* was called upon to bring rain in the event of a great drought. It was generally feared that some of their people had done

DRAWING BY KAHONHES, A MODERN INDIAN ARTIST,
OF THE IROQUOIS SNOW SNAKE GAME.

some great wrong and the Great Spirit was so angry he withheld rain as punishment.

After the special council was opened with speeches, there was a thanksgiving dance and then the *Ah-dó-weh* were introduced. These were a succession of short speeches made by different persons returning thanks to various objects and persons for acts of kindness, for their own personal achievements, and for political events. Each person followed his speech with an appropriate song which he had composed. All the people joined in a chorus as a united anthem of praise.

At a designated time after the Ah-dó-weh, which could continue for as long as two hours, the "Keeper of the Faith," who had been appointed, went to the fire and laid on his leaves of tobacco. Then he made this invocation to Hé-no, the Thunderer, as the smoke ascended:

Hé-no, our grandfather, listen now to the words of thy grandchildren. We feel grieved. Our minds are sorely troubled. We fear our supporters will fail and bring famine upon us. We ask our grandfather that he may come, and give us rain, that the earth may not dry up, land refuse to produce for our support. Thy grandchildren all send their salutations to their grandfather, Hé-no.

Then the Keeper of the Faith would take another handful of tobacco and offer a similar prayer to Hä-wen-né-yu, the Great Spirit.

Among the Algonquian-speaking Delawares the universe was controlled by four powerful manitous or assistants to the Great Spirit: In the east, "Our grandfather — where daylight appears," in the west, "Our grandfather — where the sun goes down," in the south, "Our grandfather — where it is warm," and in the north, "Our grandfather — where it is winter." The sun and moon were called, "Our elder brothers," and the Delawares believed that the thunderers were manlike beings who brought rain to protect mankind from the onslaught of water monsters. "Our mother earth" cared for and fed the people and "Living-Solid-Face," whose head was supposed to be of solid wood, lived in the forest and had charge of the wild game. But the Great Spirit ruled over all and lived in the topmost tier of the heaven which was supposed to consist of twelve layers, each layer inhabited by various spirits. Among the

Wampanoags there was a special god, *Squauanit* for women and *Much-qua-chuck* for children.

The Algonquians called their priests *Powwows*. The priests performed and managed their worship. The word "powwow" today means a gathering or meeting.

The Green Corn Festival of the eastern woodland Indians was a three-day ceremony during which prayers and dances of thanksgiving were offered.

In 1799 a new Iroquoian religion was founded by a Seneca sachem named *Gä-ne-o-dí-yo* or Handsome Lake. He was born at the Indian village of *Gä-no-waú-ges* near present-day Avon, New York, about 1735 and died at Onondaga in 1815. He was a member of the Turtle clan and a half-brother of a famous Indian chief named Cornplanter. Handsome Lake was an elderly man when in 1793 he lay ill, presumably dying from, among other things, the effects of a hard-drinking life. As he lay on his sickbed, he had a dream in which he had a vision of emissaries from the Great Spirit. They told him that, because of his devotion to the Great Spirit, he would be cured of his illness and that the next day he should ask his people to assemble so that Handsome Lake could reveal his message from the Great Spirit. In this message he said:

> Your Creator has seen that you have transgressed greatly against His laws. He made man pure and good. He did not intend that he should sin. You commit a great sin in taking the firewater. The Great Spirit says that you must abandon this enticing habit. Your ancestors have brought great misery and suffering upon you. They first took the firewater of the white man and entailed upon you its consequences. None of them has gone to heaven. The firewater does not belong to you. It was made for the white man beyond the great waters. . . . The Great Spirit says that drunkenness is a great crime and He forbids you to indulge in this evil habit. . . .

Handsome Lake also extolled the virtues of faithfulness in marriage, the love of parents for children, that children should obey their parents — for, he said, "Disobedient children cause great pain and misery." He also said that those women who could not have children of their own should adopt orphans and care for poor children. He also cautioned families to live in love and harmony. The most important facet of Handsome Lake's teachings was that it was the beginning of a temperance movement within the League of the Iroquois and did much to reform his people. Many of the Iroquois Indians today still practice the religion of Handsome Lake and many of the young people are embracing Handsome Lake's "new religion." It has had a powerful effect upon the life and mores of the Iroquois nations. This quotation expresses the philosophy of Handsome Lake: "Life is uncertain, therefore, while we live, let us love each other. Let us sympathize always with the suffering and the needy. Let us always rejoice with those who are glad."

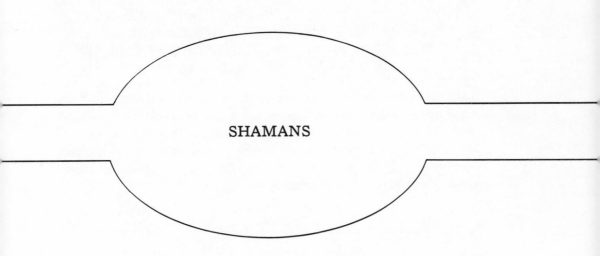

SHAMANS

Belief in the supernatural was very strong among northeastern Indian tribes. Certain individuals who were believed to have especially strong supernatural powers were called *shamans*. Shamans were also referred to as "medicine men" but they did a great deal more than just cure the sick.

Shamans were believed to be able to make direct contact with the spirit world and therefore they were presumed to be able to call for aid from a supernatural spirit. Sometimes the shamans themselves were thought to be possessed of spirits. Shamans were believed able to intercede with the spirit world on the part of an individual or groups of individuals, such as a tribe. The success of a hunt, good crops, or warfare were believed to hinge to a great degree on the exhortations of the shaman to the spirit world.

As medicine men shamans on occasion were called upon to heal white colonists when there was no white doctor available. Many times Indian herbal medicines were exploited by unscrupulous white medicine men who gave them phoney labels such as "kickapoo juice." Sometimes these white medicine men made extravagant claims that their Indian medicines could cure anything from warts to appendicitis. Shamans among the eastern woodlands Indians frequently exercised great power within the tribe. Sometimes they were no more than talented magicians.

A secret society among the eastern woodlands Indians called *Midewiwin* or Grand Medicine Society was founded originally to heal the sick by spiritual means. The society had many special rituals, songs, and initiation ceremonies with a series of grades or degrees, much like the white man's Masonic Lodge. The eventual gain of considerable political power caused so much trouble with various tribes that those tribes outlawed it. Today on many reservations the shaman or medicine man still exists and many Indians adhere to the old beliefs of his supernatural power and hold the shaman in great respect.

MYTHS AND LEGENDS

All Indian tribes have legends handed down from generation to generation. Some of these legends are the stories of famous chiefs or warriors, but many of the legends dwell on the supernatural. This is one Iroquois legend:

A young girl who lived at *Gä'-u-ġwa,* a village above Niagara Falls at the mouth of Cayuga Creek, had been betrothed to a disagreeable old man. She ran away and decided to end her life by going over the falls in a canoe. As the canoe went over the great cataract, the young Indian girl disappeared although the canoe was found swirling about in the currents below. Before she reached the waters underneath, she was caught in a blanket by Hé-no, the Thunderer, and his two assistants and carried to Hé-no's home behind the falls. She later was married to one of Hé-no's children.

Now her people in the Indian village had suffered from an annual pestilence. Hé-no told the young girl the reason for the pestilence and sent her back to her people to explain how the pestilence could be cured. Hé-no said that there was a monstrous serpent who lived under the village and whose food consisted of the bodies of the buried dead Indians. In order to have plenty of bodies to eat, he poisoned the waters of the Niagara and the Cayuga Creek so that the people would die. The girl told her people to move to the Buffalo Creek. After the people left, the great serpent put his head above the ground to see what had happened to the source of his food. He found that the village was deserted. He followed the scent of the people and went up to Buffalo Creek. While he was in the narrow channel of the creek, Hé-no let loose with a terrific thunderbolt which killed the monster. The huge body of the serpent floated downstream and lodged upon the edge of the great cataract. A part of the body arched backward near the northern shore forming a semicircle. The raging waters dammed up by the body broke through the rocks behind and this [say the Seneca Indians] is how the Horseshoe Falls at Niagara Falls was formed.

The Penobscots of Maine, an Algonquian people, were among those who practiced *totem*. This meant that each family had a particular animal as its emblem. People believed that they were descended from the particular animal or from a legendary ancestor who was associated with the particular animal. The word "totem" comes from the Algonquian Ojibwas and means "He is my relative." There were two kinds of totems among the Penobscot — the freshwater and the saltwater. Frog and Eel were freshwater totems, while Whale, Crab, Sturgeon, and Lobster were saltwater totems. Every Penobscot explained their association by the same myth:

Many, many generations ago, a giant frog swallowed all the world's water. This caused a great drought, but a hero slew the frog and released the water. Some of the thirsty people foolishly rushed into the water and were transformed into various saltwater animals. The relatives who survived them took the names of the aquatic animals into which members of their families had been transformed.

The Algonquians were great believers in charms and very often traded them at high prices to other Indian tribes. One Algonquian charm was supposed to bring fishing luck. Some pretty girls were chosen from the tribe and formally "married" to the tribal fishing nets. This was supposed to please the Fish Spirit as the girls were to be his brides. To show his appreciation, the Fish Spirit was supposed to see that the nets of the tribe were always filled full of fishes when they were drawn from the water.

The Indians are a poetic people and much of their old poetry has been translated into English. One such poem of the Passamaquoddys is the "Song of the Stars":

We are the stars which sing,
We sing with our light;
We are the birds of fire,
We fly over the sky.
Our light is a voice;
We make a road for spirits,
For the spirits to pass over.
Among us are three hunters
Who chase a bear;
There never was a time
When they were not hunting.
We look down on the mountains.
This is the song of the stars.

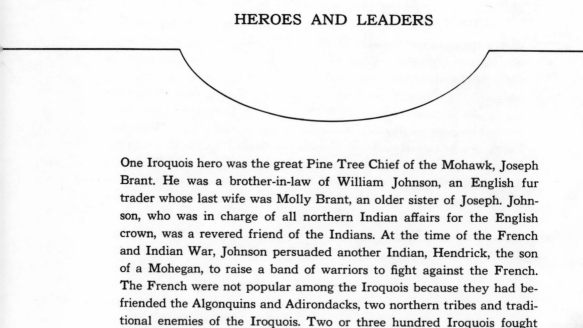

HEROES AND LEADERS

One Iroquois hero was the great Pine Tree Chief of the Mohawk, Joseph Brant. He was a brother-in-law of William Johnson, an English fur trader whose last wife was Molly Brant, an older sister of Joseph. Johnson, who was in charge of all northern Indian affairs for the English crown, was a revered friend of the Indians. At the time of the French and Indian War, Johnson persuaded another Indian, Hendrick, the son of a Mohegan, to raise a band of warriors to fight against the French. The French were not popular among the Iroquois because they had befriended the Algonquins and Adirondacks, two northern tribes and traditional enemies of the Iroquois. Two or three hundred Iroquois fought in the decisive Battle of Lake George under Johnson and Hendrick. Hendrick was killed and Iroquois casualties were very heavy. Colonel Johnson became Sir William Johnson and took over the education of his young brother-in-law, Joseph Brant, who had fought at Lake George as a thirteen-year-old warrior.

Joseph was sent to an Indian school conducted by the Reverend Eleazar Wheelock in Connecticut. He received an education, particularly a religious one, and later helped missionaries to translate parts of the Bible into the Mohegan language. During the American Revolution, because of Brant's friendship with the British, he wanted the Iroquois people to fight on the English side. The Revolution ended the power of the great League of the Iroquois, as most of the Mohawk, Onondaga, Cayuga, and Seneca fought on the British side, while the Tuscaroras and Oneidas sided with the American colonies. Brant and his followers were granted lands in Canada's Ontario province, while those who were loyal to the American cause remained in New York.

Certainly one of the most famous of the Algonquian Indians was *Massasoit*, the great sachem of the Wampanoag federation. Massasoit was born in 1580 and became sachem of the Wampanoag federation in 1607. At one time before his people were raided by the fierce Tarratines, a tribe of the Abenakis, there were 25,000 people in his federation. After the plague in or before the year 1616, there were fewer than seven thousand of his people left alive. Massasoit signed a treaty with the English Pilgrims which stipulated that Massasoit or any of his people would not injure the English. The Pilgrims in turn promised they would not hurt Massasoit's people and if any Englishman did, he would be turned over to Massasoit for punishment. The treaty also included a mutual assistance clause providing that Massasoit would aid the English if they were attacked and the English likewise would send their soldiers to protect him if he were under attack. Massasoit remained faithful and helpful to the English and was deeply mourned when he died. Massasoit's youngest son, *Sun-cone-whew*, through the influence of the Reverend John Eliot, was educated at Harvard College. This young man was a brother of Metacomet, known as King Philip, and was killed during King Philip's War in 1675.

Squanto, another famous Algonquian Indian, was born between 1575 and 1580 in Pawtuxet, Massachusetts, or what is known today as

THE GREAT PINE TREE CHIEF
OF THE MOHAWK, JOSEPH BRANT.

Plymouth. He was one of five eastern woodlands Indians kidnapped by Captain George Weymouth and taken to England in 1605. He was given over to Sir Ferdinando Gorges who hoped to found several settlements in New England. In England Squanto learned to speak English and was eventually returned to New England and given his freedom. He was captured a second time by Captain Thomas Hunt and taken to Malaga, Spain, where he was sold as a slave. Squanto escaped and made his way back to England where he was befriended by an Englishman, John Slanie, a wealthy merchant. He finally reached his home in New England only to find that his tribe had been completely wiped out by a plague. Because of Squanto's familiarity with the English language, he was influential with the British and consequently served as their interpreter. Squanto died near Chatham, Massachusetts, during an expedition with Governor William Bradford to search for food for the white settlers among the Cape Cod Indians.

These were just a few of the many famous Indian leaders and warriors.

WOODLAND MUSIC AND ART

The main instrument of the Indians was the rawhide drum. This drum was about the size of a washtub and was painted half red, half blue with a yellow stripe which represented the path of the sun. The drum was suspended from wooden stakes, never allowed to touch the ground, and the stakes were heavily beaded and decorated with pieces of metal and fur. Underneath the drum was a blanket or large piece of colored cloth. During the Drum or Dream Dance, four drummers sat around the drum and its sounds were supposed to carry messages to the Great Spirit. A smaller hand drum was used during war dances and the mocassin game and sometimes by medicine men. Those Indians who lived in the woods also had a unique drum called a water drum. The top of the drum was tan buckskin which was held in place by a wooden rim. The bottom of the drum was solid. About two to three inches of water was contained

THE DECORATED DRUM USED IN THE DRUM OR DREAM DANCE;
THE SHORTER HAND DRUM AND TALLER WATER DRUM;
BIRCHBARK, HORN, AND TURTLE SHELL RATTLES.

ONONDAGA FALSE FACE SOCIETY DANCERS.

within the drum and shaken to wet the skin head. This produced a muted sound. The drum was used in many ceremonies.

Birch bark, buffalo or steer horns, and turtle shells were used as rattles much as Latin Americans used the maraca. The Iroquois called such instruments "singing tools" and the Seneca referred to them as "those things used for propping up songs."

In ceremonies such as the Sun Dance, a whistle made of eagle bone was used. The flute, blown at one end like today's recorder, was another instrument the Indians had and sometimes it was used by young men in their courtship. Notched sticks were rubbed against each other to make a rasping sound.

Many of the Algonquian tribes were expert basket makers, using plain plaiting of hardwood splints. Sometimes the splints were dyed and sometimes designs were painted on them. Soft diagonally plaited bags of cedar bark were used to store wild rice. Sometimes wild sweet grasses were used in the making of baskets. The Iroquois also made baskets from ash splints. Some of their most common baskets were corn-washers, baskets for berry picking, and sieves.

Feathers were widely used by the eastern woodland Indians. A headband of stiff tail and wing feathers was used by the Penobscot and other Algonquian peoples. Topknots of feathers mounted on caps were worn by the Iroquois. We have mentioned before the use of feathers to make capes by the Algonquians. The use of porcupine quills dyed with natural vegetable dyes was popular among eastern woodland Indians. The quillwork was done by wrapping or folding quills around a single thread which was then sewn to the cloth or skin. Many beautiful and intricate designs were made on dresses, moccasins, belts, and bags. The quillwork was native to the Indian craftsman, and the beadwork and ribbon appliques which one sees on the costumes of the Indians in museums was done with materials from white traders.

The beadwork of the eastern woodland Indian gave a lacy effect. The Iroquois embossed their beading by using a kind of lazy stitch where the beads were crowded and the designs raised with padding.

Wood carving, although usually associated with the Indians of the northwest coast of the United States, was also a fine art among eastern woodland Indians. Many handsome wooden carved masks were used by the Iroquois in healing ceremonies. Sometimes, particularly among the Mohawk, a doting father might do beautiful and intricate carvings on the back of his baby's cradleboard.

Around 1800 the Iroquois began to make brooches, bracelets, earrings, and other pieces of jewelry from silver. Coins and ingots were hammered into sheets and decorated by stamping or rouletting (making dots, slits, or perforations as decorations).

Dancing was another expression of art and music. The dancers many times used lavishly decorated costumes and carved masks. Sometimes the dances told a story as part of a particular ceremony or ritual. Some dances were happy ones and some depicted sad moments such as mourning.

THE WHITE MAN ARRIVES TO STAY AND CONQUER

Quite possibly the first Europeans to reach North American shores were the Vikings, the fierce seafaring men of Scandinavia. We do know that in 1006 Leif Ericsson's brother, Thorwald, came ashore somewhere on the northeastern coast and attacked and killed eight Indians.

Giovanni da Verrazano, a sixteenth-century explorer from Florence, Italy, came to the New England coast in 1524 and kidnapped a young Indian boy and took him to France. The following year the Indians had their revenge because Verrazano, on his return to America, was captured and killed by an Indian tribe.

Although the Indians usually treated the visiting white explorers with courtesy and hospitality, they were often repaid by treachery. For instance, a French explorer, Jacques Cartier, visited an Indian village where he was feasted and given gifts of large bundles of furs. When he was ready to leave, he abducted the Indian chief and eight other impor-

(57)

tant men of the tribe. They died soon after their arrival in France. When Cartier returned to the same tribe, he told them that the chief had died but that the eight men had married French noblewomen and were living in luxury. The Indians refused to believe this tale and showed their displeasure in true Indian fashion — by refusing to fraternize with the Frenchmen or to supply food and trading goods. Some of Cartier's men died of scurvy and Cartier was forced to abandon the trading post and return to France.

In 1603 the French explorer Samuel de Champlain had already established a trading post at the mouth of the St. Lawrence River in Canada, but sailed south to New England to find food and more suitable headquarters where the winters were less severe. He visited Boston Harbor and Plymouth, Massachusetts, where he was cordially entertained by the Pawtuxets. Champlain's friendly visit ended in a shooting incident at Nauset Harbor when the Indians snatched a large iron kettle from the sailors and ran into the woods. The sailors chased the culprits into the woods and were all killed by a barrage of arrows.

The countries primarily interested in exploration and colonization of North America were England, France, Spain, and to a lesser degree, the Netherlands. Exaggerated tales of great treasures including gold, silver, and other precious metals plus furs and the fabled Fountain of Youth inspired many adventurous spirits and even great governments to equip and finance expeditions to the New World. Although perhaps many of the explorers were in search of adventure, many more came out of greed to line their own pockets and to achieve fame and honors at the courts of their kings and queens. One of the most important motives was to find a northwest passage to China. Of course, New England explorers did not find gold, but cod fishing was almost as lucrative as gold mines. The profit from the fur trade led to great fleets of trading ships on the New England coast. Their number before 1620 is estimated to be from one hundred and fifty to two hundred and fifty ships a year.

Several Algonquian tribes inhabited Manhattan, New Jersey, and Long Island when the early Dutch settlers led by Henry Hudson arrived and later sailed up the Hudson River. Attitudes of the Europeans toward the Indians differed. The Dutch considered them savages and by

A CONTEMPORARY DRAWING OF CHAMPLAIN
AND HIS SAILORS SURPRISED BY THE INDIANS.

ALGONQUIANS OF THE HUDSON RIVER VALLEY AT
THE TIME HENRY HUDSON SAILED UP THE RIVER.

and large treated them with contempt. For example, the Dutch historian De Laete, in a book entitled *The New World*, published in 1624, gave this description of the Indians:

> The Indians are indolent, and some, crafty and wicked, having slain several of our people. The Manhattans [this is a misnomer, for there was no tribe called Manhattan], a fierce nation, occupy the eastern bank of the river near its mouth. Though hostile to our people, they have sold them the island or point of land which is separated from the main by Hellegat, and there they laid the foundations of a city called New Amsterdam.
>
> The barbarians are divided into many nations and languages but differ little in manners. . . . They worship a being called Manetto, are governed by chiefs called Sagamos, are suspicious, timid, revengeful and fickle, but hospitable when well treated, ready to serve the white man for little compensation.

Many of the Dutch settlers took full advantage of Indian hospitality but returned it by wanton killing of even women and children. This behavior led to acts of revenge on the part of the Indian which, due to the superior strength and firearms of the Dutch, resulted in the massacre of thousands of Indians.

The Indian regarded the land as a sacred trust from the Great Spirit and many Indians who "sold" land to the white man did not fully understand the nature of the transaction. They believed they were only giving the rights to use the land, but never envisioned they would be expelled from it as eventually happened.

Many of the English Pilgrims and other religious groups who came to New England to seek religious freedom and a new homeland seemed to have had true respect for the Indians and treated them with fairness, although there are many instances where Englishmen needlessly slaughtered Indians and by acts of violence provoked the Indians to war upon them.

There were two major seventeenth-century New England Indian wars — the Pequot War of 1637 and King Philip's War of 1675-1677. Understanding and trust between Indians and whites was at best tenuous.

There was always an undercurrent of mistrust. By 1636 emigration to the New World had swelled and there were constant incursions by whites on Indian lands. These later arrivals to New England had little understanding of the Indians and treated them high-handedly, which inflamed Indian tempers. In 1637 Massachusetts Bay Puritans, angered by an alleged Pequot attack on some white men, proceeded to destroy a Pequot town. This led to a short but savage war in which the whites were aided by Mohegans and Narragansetts, both enemies of the Pequots. Puritan clergymen considered the Pequots as agents of Satan, which gave impetus to the Puritans in their determination to crush the Indians. This they did with a vengeance, setting on fire the principal Pequot town near the Mystic River in Connecticut and roasting to death or shooting more than six hundred Indians.

From that time on, and following the death of Massasoit in 1661, anti-Indian feeling increased and the former good relations between Massachusetts settlers and the Wampanoags ended. This breakdown in relations led Massasoit's son, *Metacomet*, or King Philip, to try to form an alliance of northeastern tribes. He even tried to enlist help of the Iroquois Mohawks of New York. King Philip was only twenty-four years old when he became chief sachem of the Wampanoags. He was especially able, proud, statesmanlike, and a past master at outwitting the English. For many years the English lived under the threat of war from King Philip as he tried, largely unsuccessfully, to form an alliance with other tribes. Old tribal jealousies and distrust of his motives by other chiefs frustrated his efforts.

But despite these frustrations, war erupted in 1675. Philip's initial success persuaded some tribes, including the Nipmucs of Massachusetts and the Narragansetts to join him. Several successful attacks on white towns from the Connecticut River to Massachusetts and Narragansett Bay took place. At least fifty-two of the ninety white settlements in New England suffered attacks and twelve were completely destroyed. For a time it looked as though the Indians might defeat the colonists. However, this was not to be. A year after the beginning of the war the Indians ran short of food and many defected from Philip's army. Other Indians who were friendly to the whites aided and abetted them and with the help of an

CONSTANT INCURSIONS BY SETTLERS
ON INDIAN LANDS BROUGHT WAR TO
SEVENTEENTH-CENTURY NEW ENGLAND.

THE GREAT SACHEM OF THE WAMPANOAG,
KING PHILIP OR METACOMET

Indian informer, Philip was killed. After Philip's death, hundreds of his people surrendered thinking they would be granted amnesty, but instead many were executed, while others were sold into slavery. Some of those who escaped fled westward and were killed by unfriendly Indians while others were allowed to join western tribes. A few of the veterans of King Philip's War went to Maine and joined forces with the Abenakis. Individual bands of Indians were finally wiped out and Indian power in the Northeast became a matter of history. Today only a few hundred Indians live in New England.

The third large-scale disaster among the Algonquian Indians was a brutal massacre in Westchester County. William Kieft, the fifth governor of the New Netherlands Colony (New York), and a Dutchman, led a frightful massacre against the Weckquaesgeeks and Tappans in 1643 and succeeded in burning and destroying their villages and killing most of the population.

For the most part, the white man considered the Indian a useful adjunct to his colonization, but a necessary evil to be put to his own use and basically expendable. However, not all white men felt this way. Although intermarriage with Indians was the exception and generally frowned upon, there were those who did marry Indian wives and through them came to love and respect their wives' people. One such man was Sir William Johnson, who married a Mohawk, Molly Brant, the sister of Joseph Brant. Johnson was very impressed with the demeanor of the Six Nations of the Iroquois during the Grand Council meeting at Onondaga. He wrote to a friend in England that the speaker was never interrupted, harsh language was never used no matter what the speaker may have been thinking at the time. Johnson believed that many Englishmen were ignorant of Indian customs and believed that if their culture were better understood they would be admired and respected by the white men. A young British military officer, Charles Lee, wrote to his sister in England, describing the Iroquois:

I can assure you that they are a much better sort of people than commonly represented; they are hospitable, friendly and civil to an immense degree. In good breeding I think they infinitely surpass the

French or any other people that I ever saw. If you will allow good breeding to consist in the constant desire to do ev'rything that will please you, and in strict carefulness not to do anything that may offend you. . . . (These warriors acquire something of an ease and gracefulness in their walk and air which is not to be met with elsewhere.) Their Dress I like most wonderfully. . . . Their Complexion is deep olive, their eyes and teeth very fine, but their skins are most inexpressibly soft and silky. Their men in general are handsomer than their women, but I have seen some of them very pretty.

One attitude which was bound to create trouble between Indian and white was the desperate attempt the white man made to make the Indians submit to a white way of life, including religion, farming, and hunting.

The last words of the Walum Olum are:

At this time, from North and South the whites came.
They are peaceful;
They have great things;
Who are they?

It was not long before the Indians found out.

TREATIES WITH THE INDIANS

The white man has made many treaties with Indian tribes, but few have been kept to the letter. Indeed, it is this fact which is largely responsible for the resentment today's American Indians harbor against the white man. In almost all instances, the Indians signed their treaties in good faith and they reasonably expected good faith from the white man.

When the English began to colonize, the king of England granted vast tracts of land to the settlers, many times in recognition of service to the king and with little or no regard for the Indians. In fact, the British attitude, and one which has persisted into the twentieth century is that, "to the victor belong the spoils." In other words, a country which colonizes thereby gains rights to the land without regard to the property rights of the native population.

One of the earliest treaties was the Pettaquamscut Treaty negotiated with the Narragansetts on July 15, 1675. This treaty was at the conclusion of King Philip's War and its terms were particularly harsh. British officers, led by Major Thomas Savage and representing the colonies of Massachusetts and Connecticut, demanded that the Narragansett sachems were to deliver to the British all of King Philip's subjects "dead or alive." They also demanded that all "stolen property" was to be returned to the white man, that pilfering and "acts of hostility" toward the English shall for the future forever cease. In addition, a certain number of chiefs were demanded as hostages to insure the peace. The reward for the capture of King Philip was two coats, and for his head, one coat. All land grants, sales, bargains, conveyances of land, meadow, timber, grass, or stone which had been bought or simply taken over by the English were renewed or confirmed forever. The terms of this treaty hardly endeared the white man to the Indians and when they did not live up to the letter of the treaty, a vicious attack was launched against the Indians. It has been suggested that the attack by the white men was based upon "the theory of preventive war" and the potential market value of Narragansett land.

Eventually grants of land were made to the Indians in the New England area, but whether by design or unthinkingly, taxes were levied on these lands. This was an item which the Indians neither expected nor fully understood. In time, of course, the land was seized by the States for back taxes and the Indians found themselves once again dispossessed. There are a few reservations in New England, two in the state of Maine for example, but for the most part, New England Indians today live in white communities, although they may group together to form a small settlement such as Mashpee on Cape Cod.

This does not mean that they have willingly or completely assimilated into the white culture. Many of the younger Indians are demanding a return of Indian lands for their own use. The likelihood of success of the Indian cause seems remote, but the fact of the bitterness and resentment toward the white man is likely to remain unless some compromise can be worked out. Many white people feel that there are so few New England Indians left that the problem can easily be ignored.

Of the original 18,000,000 acres of land belonging to the League of the Iroquois, only 78,000 acres are today in Indian hands. Prior to the

EUROPEAN SETTLERS "PURCHASING"
LANDS FROM THE INDIANS.

A TUSCARORA VILLAGE IN 1876:
THE CHIEF'S HOUSE, THE CHIEF, INTERIOR
OF A HOME, AND THE SCHOOL HOUSE.

American Revolution, the British set forth a royal proclamation in 1763 providing that the Appalachian watershed was to be the western boundary of land open to colonial expansion. In other words, anything west of that line, which ran from Fort Stanwix on Lake Ontario all the way down to south of Tryon, North Carolina, was considered Indian land and could not be expropriated by the white man. However, by the end of the American Revolution, the cry of "Westward Ho" was being heard and fifty years later that cry would become a roar. It was reasonable that the Indians, if they were to survive at all, would have to make concessions and give way to the superior strength and numbers of the new Americans. On October 22, 1784, another treaty was concluded by three United States commissioners, Oliver Wolcott, Richard Butler, and Arthur Lee and the sachems and warriors of the Six Nations. Article I said that six hostages would be taken by the United States until all prisoners were released by the Indians. Remember that except for the Oneidas and Tuscaroras, the tribes of the Six Nations sided with their traditional friends, the British, during the Revolution. Article II stated that the Oneidas and Tuscaroras should be "secured in the possession of lands on which they are settled." Article III defined the boundaries of Indian lands and, in short, meant the Indians relinquished their rights to lands west of the Ohio River.

Many Indians of the Six Nations settled or were driven into Canada. Most of these, including Mohawks, Oneidas, Onondagas, and Cayugas, are in eastern Quebec and southern Ontario, although there is a small migrant group of Iroquois numbering less than two hundred who voyaged as far as Edmonton, Alberta. There is an Onondaga reservation near Syracuse, New York. Today life for members of the Six Nations is not much rosier than for native Americans anywhere. The Iroquois people from the northern New York areas were spared the humiliation of being forcibly removed from their homelands to unfamiliar territory as were the Cherokees and other tribes to the south.

As early as 1742, Indians began to see the writing on the wall and to realize that they were fighting a losing battle with the white man for possession of their lands. At that time, *Canessatego*, a sachem of the Six Nations, said:

(71)

We know our Lands are now become more Valuable. The white People think we do not know their Value, but we are sensible that the Land is Everlasting and a few Goods we receive for it are soon Worn out and Gone.

He also complained that the grazing of cows and horses was creating a scarcity of food for deer, a main source of meat to the Indian.

Eventually the United States government concluded that it would be best to have the majority of Indians in one area which would be designated "Indian territory." On May 28, 1830, legislation was passed which provided for territory west of the Mississippi to be given to the Indians in perpetuity. It was claimed that this land was in exchange for lands held in the southeastern United States such as Cherokee land in the Carolinas.

Today the descendants of the League of the Iroquois are concentrated in upstate New York and southeastern Canada. The Six Nations Tribal Council still meets and its people try to preserve traditional ways and attitudes. Conditions on the New York State and eastern Canadian reservations are not much of an improvement, if any, over the plight of their brother tribes in the rest of the United States and Canada. Much of the land is poor and little aid has been afforded the Indian to enhance his fortunes.

RESERVATION LIFE TODAY

Eventually the white man grudgingly assigned some lands to the Indians which are known as reservations. Today in all parts of the United States where there are Indians, many are still living on reservations, although others have tried to adjust to urban life and live in cities and towns.

Poverty, degradation, substandard housing, lack of modern facilities, poor schools, and generally run-down conditions are prevalent on Indian reservations. Many times the land given by treaty to the Indians as reservations is of poor quality and yields little in the way of sustenance. Frequently the better reservation land has been leased to white profiteers and so yields the Indians very little. Unemployment among Indians is high, for educational facilities are limited. The average income of eastern Indians living on reservations is far below the national average.

There are some Indian men, such as the Mohawks, who have become famed as steelworkers on construction sites because of their extraordinary sense of balance. These Indians are well paid for their skilled work, but the urban life is ill-suited to their spiritual and emotional needs and very often they find city living impossible.

Despite the growing interest in the plight of the American Indians and their culture, history, religion, and legend, there still exists today a large segment of prejudiced people. The urban Indians pay for this attitude in crowded living conditions and ostracism from the mainstream of American urban life. The Indians are sensitive, generous, and warm-hearted individuals. They will answer friendship with friendship, but they can be mortally wounded by betrayal or insensitivity to their own beliefs. Indians are still considered by some Americans to be a shiftless, indolent, dirty, and drunken bunch. Young adult Indians today are working hard to erase this stereotype.

One example of incredible prejudice against the Indian is the story of Eli Samuel Parker (*Donehogawa*), Keeper of the Western Door of the longhouse of the Iroquois. As an ambitious young man on the Seneca-Tonawanda reservation, Parker realized that he had a better chance of success if he took an anglicized name. As a very young boy he worked on an army post as a stable boy. The officers teased him because of his poor command of English, so he determined to learn English as well as any white man. This he did at a missionary school. After finishing school he decided the best way to help his people was to study law. In those days, the middle 1800s, a man became a lawyer by working in a lawyer's office and then taking the state bar examination. Eli Parker, when he applied for admittance to the bar, was told that only white male citizens could practice law in New York. No Indian need apply. This snub did not deter Parker's determination. He entered Rensselaer Polytechnic Institute and became a civil engineer.

He got a United States government job supervising construction of levees and buildings in Galena, Illinois, and made friends with a white clerk in a harness store. This harness salesman was a former army captain named Ulysses S. Grant. At the beginning of the Civil War Parker went back to New York to try to raise an Iroquois regiment to fight on the Union side under Grant. Again he met with prejudice, for the governor of New York told him there was no place for Indians in the New

MOHAWK WARRIORS IN 1869.
AT THE RIGHT IS SIMCOE KERR,
GRANDSON OF JOSEPH BRANT.

ELI SAMUEL PARKER
OR DONEHOGAWA.

York Volunteers. Parker then went to Washington to offer his service as an engineer to the War Department. Although the Union army was sorely in need of trained engineers, they refused to accept Indian engineers. Parker was informed that the Civil War was a white man's war.

After meeting with these rebuffs, Parker returned to the Tonawanda reservation but wrote his old friend Ulysses S. Grant, now General Grant, explaining his predicament. After fighting government bureaucracy, General Grant managed to send for Eli Samuel Parker to join him at Vicksburg. Eli Parker attained the rank of lieutenant colonel and when General Robert E. Lee surrendered at Appomattox, Lieutenant Colonel Parker was asked by General Grant to write the terms of surrender because of Parker's superior penmanship. Eventually Parker was promoted to brigadier general and when Grant was elected president of the United States, he chose Parker to be commissioner of Indian Affairs.

Although Eli Parker was born more than a hundred years ago, it is not uncommon in certain parts of the country today for an Indian to be refused employment or housing simply because he is an Indian. Modern laws promoting equal opportunities have not totally wiped out racial discrimination.

INDIAN POWER

Today there is a strong movement among young Indians to force the United States government to make retribution for broken treaties and to pay debts which it still owes various Indian tribes. There are several Indian organizations pursuing this goal.

The first militant sign of Indian activism took place in 1964. During the years of the Eisenhower administration, the Department of the Interior, which has the government responsibility for Indian welfare, began to develop programs to move Indians from their reservations into midwestern and Pacific coast cities. The result of this philosophy was disastrous. A generation of Indian children grew up in substandard housing in urban centers where Indian job opportunities were almost nonexistent. Medical services were refused by city officials because they felt the Indians should return to the reservation to be cared for by United States public health medical services.

By 1964 the tenseness between Indian and white had increased and

TOM PORTER,
YOUNG MOHAWK LEADER.

Indian resentment of rejection was bitter. When the government abandoned Alcatraz Island as a federal prison, two young Sioux Indians from South Dakota who were living in the San Francisco Bay area landed on the island and claimed it as Indian land under an 1868 Sioux treaty, perhaps the first sign of militant Indian activism in recent years. The Indian takeover of Alcatraz, although finally unsuccessful, put the plight of the Indians into national newspaper headlines. Although scattered groups of Indians managed to remain on the island until the summer of 1971, they were finally surprised by federal marshals and forcefully taken off the island.

By the summer of 1972 tensions again were mounting among Indian tribes. Several Indians, including Richard Oakes, leader of the Alcatraz movement, were shot to death. In mid-September Indians met in Denver, Colorado, and formed a caravan which they called the "Trail of Broken Treaties." Their plan was to form a massive march on Washington to present their grievances to the government and to obtain retribution. Several sections of the caravan proceeded from different points in the country, picking up Indians, young and old, men, women, and children. Although the government had known of the caravan for several weeks, it made few, if any, plans to accommodate the many hundreds of Indians destined for Washington. The outcome of this ill-fated march was a takeover of the Interior Department's Bureau of Indian Affairs offices. Although this dramatic step by Indians afforded them coverage by national press, radio, and television, there were few concrete gains.

In the spring of 1973, a group of militant leaders took over the town of Wounded Knee on the Oglala Sioux reservation in South Dakota. Again the Indians tried to force recognition of their grievances upon government officials. The Indians barricaded themselves at Wounded Knee and defied federal authorities, saying they were willing to die in the cause of their people. At the conclusion of the Wounded Knee takeover agreements were signed which have yet to be carried out, and many of the Indian leaders, such as Russell Means, an articulate and able Sioux and a leader of the American Indian Movement (AIM), along with several other Indians, were to be tried in federal court. In 1974, the case was dismissed.

LOOKING INTO THE FUTURE

There are positive aspects in Indian life today. Many more colleges and universities are offering scholarships for Indian students, but sometimes even a full scholarship will not afford an Indian a college education unless money is raised for travel, clothing, and living expenses. Sometimes the wealthier tribes, such as the Navajos, can provide needed funds for outstanding students. But most tribes are much too poor, so the money must be raised through private sources. The government does provide some scholarship money for deserving students and there are various Indian organizations and biracial groups which help to finance Indian students.

Although many Indians today live in urban centers and a few are successfully pursuing careers, many more in the cities are destitute. Among young Indians there is a revival of the teaching of the old ways of their religion, tribal customs, and ceremonies. Today's young Indians

PRIZE-WINNING STONE SCULPTURE
OF TO-DO-DA-HO, AN
EVIL SPIRIT WHO LIVED BEFORE
THE IROQUOIS CONFEDERACY,
BY DUFFY WILSON, IROQUOIS.

are proud of their heritage and are striving desperately to preserve it. There are several Indian publications published and edited in the United States. *Akwesasne Notes* is published on the Mohawk reservation and covers Indian news and activities across the United States and Canada.

Today there is a crying need for more Indian professional people such as lawyers, doctors, and teachers who can aid their people to realize full justice and equality. Julius Cook, a prominent Mohawk, best summed up the feelings of today's Indians when he said:

Today our people must have education if we are to survive. We must learn to think like the white man. But, we must also hold fast to the best elements of our own culture. If we lose the latter, we will die inside.

SELECTED READING

Akwesasne Notes, Mohawk Nation. Via Rooseveltown, N.Y.: published without charge eight times yearly by the Mohawk Nation.

Bjorklund, Karna L. *Indians of Northeastern America*. New York: Dodd, Mead & Co., 1969.

Gardner, Jeanne L. *Mary Jemison: Seneca Captive*. New York: Harcourt Brace Jovanovich, Inc., 1966.

Grant, Bruce. *American Indians: Yesterday and Today*. New York: E. P. Dutton & Co., Inc., 1960.

Hertzberg, Hazel W. *The Great Tree and the Longhouse: The Culture of the Iroquois*. New York: The Macmillan Company, 1966.

Josephy, Alvin M., Jr. *The Indian Heritage of America*. New York: Alfred A. Knopf, Inc., 1968.

LaFarge, Oliver. *The American Indian*. New York: Western Publishing Company, Inc., 1960.

Matson, Emerson N. *Longhouse Legends.* Camden, N.J.: Thomas Nelson Inc., 1968.

Morris, Richard B. *First Book of the Indian Wars.* New York: Franklin Watts, Inc., 1959.

Rich, Louise Dickinson. *King Philip's War.* New York: Franklin Watts, Inc., 1972.

Voight, Virginia. *Close to the Rising Sun: Algonquian Indian Legends.* Champaign, Ill.: Garrard Publishing Co., 1972.

Witt, Shirley H. *The Tuscaroras.* New York: The Macmillan Company, 1972.

Yellow Robe, Rose. *Album of the American Indian.* New York: Franklin Watts, Inc., 1969.

Dances of the North American Indians. Ed. Ronnie and Stu Lipner. New York: Folkways Records, FD6510.

Songs of the Iroquois Longhouse. Col. William N. Fenton. Washington, D.C.: Library of Congress Records, AAF56.

War Whoops and Medicine Songs. Col. Charles Hofmann. New York: Folkways Records, FE4381.

INDEX

Adolescents, 25
Agriculture, 16, 21, 38
Ah-dó-weh, 40
AIM. *See* American Indian Movement
Ak-we-sas-ne Notes, 83
Alcatraz Island, 80
Algonquians, 2, 5, 6, 9, 58, 61-62, 65
    art, 55; charms, 47; government, 30;
    heroes, 49, 51; life style, 19, 21-22;
    religion, 37-38, 40-41; social struc-
    ture, 10-12, 15
Algonquins, 31, 48
American Indian Movement, 80
American Revolution, 49, 71
Appalachian watershed, 71
Archaeological explorations, 1-2
Arts and crafts, 55-56
Asia, 1, 2

Bark houses, 16-17, 19
Basket making, 55

Beans, 16, 21, 38
Bill of Rights, United States, 35, 36
Brant, Joseph, 48, 49
Brant, Molly, 48, 65

Canada, 5, 49, 71, 72
Canassatego, 27, 29, 71-72
Canoes, 19
Cartier, Jacques, 57-58
Cayugas, 6, 12, 31, 49, 71
Central America, 2, 21
Champlain, Samuel de, 58
Charms, 47
Chiefs, 11, 27, 30-32, 35-36, 68
    See also Leaders
Children, 22, 25, 41
Civil War, 74, 77
Clans, 10-11, 36
Clothing and dress, 19, 22
Constitution, League of the Iroquois, 32,
    35-36